DICKENS IN AMERICA

adapted from the writings of Charles Dickens by

Nigel Gearing

"In which Mr Charles Dickens – the Inimitable 'Boz' –
will Entertain Company & Friends with an Account of his
Travels on that Illustrious Continent, his Impressions
and Prejudices, in the Years of 1842 and 1867."

OBERON BOOKS
LONDON
First published in 1998 by Oberon Books Ltd.

First published in 1998 by Oberon Books Ltd
Electronic edition published in 2013

Oberon Books Ltd
521 Caledonian Road, London N7 9RH
Tel: +44 (0) 20 7607 3637 / Fax: +44 (0) 20 7607 3629
e-mail: info@oberonbooks.com
www.oberonbooks.com

British Library Cataloguing-in-Publication Data
A catalogue record for this book is available from the British Library.

PB ISBN: 978-1-84002-066-3
E ISBN: 978-1-84943-947-3

Cover design: Andrzej Klimowski
Typography: Richard Doust

Cover photograph: Herbert Watkins, 1858
(By courtesy of the National Portrait Gallery, London)
eBook conversion by Replika Press PVT Ltd, India.

Visit www.oberonbooks.com to read more about all our books and to buy them. You will also find features, author interviews and news of any author events, and you can sign up for e-newsletters so that you're always first to hear about our new releases.

for Ros and Al

INTRODUCTION

Nigel Gearing

Charles Dickens gave no public lectures on the subject of his American travels. He did, however, give wildly popular readings from his own novels and for the text that follows I have adopted the format of these performances.

Drawn from his many letters, his speeches and – in the case of his first visit – his book "American Notes", every significant word in this text is by Dickens himself. The "insignificant" ones are largely my own, where – as discreetly as possible – I have sought to segue from one passage of Dickens's writing to another, binding these often disparate parts into a coherent whole. I have also, on occasion, added an explanatory word or two where an interesting remark might otherwise have remained obscure, and – most sparingly of all – have drawn on contemporary journalistic accounts where (e.g. in the case of the Boz Ball) Dickens's modesty might have prevented us from grasping the scale of the event.

Dickens loved a live audience and was himself a gifted amateur actor. One hopes he would appreciate the challenge to any actor here undertaking to impersonate him and thus having to "age up" some twenty-six years between Parts One and Two. Although Dickens only started his readings when already into his forties, it is necessary for our purposes to imagine him as both younger and older than this, turning thirty in 1842 and fifty-six in 1868 – though of course remaining, throughout, "Boz, the Inimitable".

Dickens in America was first performed at the Bristol Old Vic Theatre on 7th October 1998.

CHARLES DICKENS, Steven Crossley

Director, Ian Hastings

Designer, Mick Bearwish

Lighting Design, Lorraine Laybourne

Original Music, Christopher Littlewood

Stage Manager, Jo Cuthbert

~

In view of the literary interest of the piece – much of the material will be unfamiliar even to admirers of Dickens's novels – this edition is printing the text of *Dickens in America* as it was on the first day of rehearsal, before certain cuts and readjustments necessary for its staging at the Bristol Old Vic.

PART ONE

CHARLES DICKENS appears stage left, walks to his lectern, and – head thrown back, one hand in his pocket – surveys the audience.

He is thirty years old, unbearded and with light brown hair worn fashionably long. Beneath his top coat he sports an elaborate shirt and waistcoat; his watch-chains and rings confirm a slight tendency towards dandyism. His facial expressions change rapidly, his gestures are restlessly quick. He gives an overall impression of mental agility and self-confidence.

He begins.

It is our third morning at sea.

I am awakened out of my sleep by a dismal shriek from my wife, who demands to know whether there's any danger. I rouse myself and look out of bed. The water-jug is plunging and leaping like a lively dolphin; all the smaller articles are afloat, except my shoes, which are stranded on
a carpet-bag, high and dry, like a couple of coal-barges. Suddenly I see them spring into the air and behold the looking-glass, which is nailed to the wall, sticking fast upon the ceiling. At the same time the door entirely disappears and a new one is opened in the floor. Then I begin to comprehend that the state-room is standing on its head...

Ladies and gentlemen, it was the Winter of 1842, we were embarked on a steam-ship for America – I say, "we"; by this I would have you understand myself, my wife Kate and her maid Anne – and now this same steam-ship seemed to be a creature actually running of its own accord, with broken knees and failing legs,

through every variety of
hole and pitfall, and stumbling constantly.

"Steward!"

"Sir?"

"What *is* the matter? What *do* you call this?"

"Rather a heavy sea on, sir, and a head wind."

"A head wind!" The labouring of the ship in the troubled sea that day and the following nights I shall never forget... What the agitation of a steam-vessel is, on a bad winter's night in the wild Atlantic, it is impossible for the most vivid imagination to conceive. To say that she is flung down on her side in the waves, with her masts dipping into them, and that, springing up again, she rolls over on the other side, until a heavy sea strikes her with the noise of a hundred great guns, and hurls her back – that she stops, and staggers, and shivers, as though stunned, and then, with a violent throbbing at her heart, darts onward like a monster goaded into madness, to be beaten down and battered, and crushed, and leaped on by the angry sea – that thunder, lightning, hail and rain, and wind, are all in fierce contention for the mastery – that every plank has its groan, every nail its shriek, and every drop of water in the great ocean its howling voice – is nothing. To say that all is grand and all appalling and horrible in the last degree is nothing. Words cannot express it; thoughts cannot convey it. Only a dream can call it up again, in all its fury, rage and passion... And *there* is the "head wind" of that January crossing!

Next day and all days thereafter, the weather continuing obstinately and unprecedentedly bad (one night our fellow-passenger Lord Mulgrave laid a wager with other men as to who could reach his cabin first across the deck; the sea broke over the ship so violently that they were *five and twenty minutes* holding on by the handrail, drenched to the skin by every wave, and not daring to go on or come

back lest they should be washed overboard), the weather
continuing thus, I say, it was not until the fifteenth night
that we found ourselves running, as we thought, into
Halifax Harbour with – for once – little wind and a
bright moon. Down below we were playing a rubber of
whist, all in good spirits, when suddenly the ship struck
upon a bank of mud! Breakers were roaring ahead, and
the vessel driving upon the surf while rockets and burning blue lights were fired up as signals of distress. The
men – and I mean the *crew*! think of this – were kicking
off their shoes and throwing off their jackets prepara-
tory to swimming ashore; the pilot was beside himself;
the passengers dismayed; and everything in the most
intolerable confusion and hurry.

At last the boat we had sent ashore returned. Our
captain was proved quite right: in a sudden fog and
through the pilot's folly we had got into a place called
the Eastern-passage. Here, surrounded by rocks and
shoals of all kinds, we had happily drifted into a perfect
little pond... and,
it seemed, the only safe speck in the place.

Ladies and gentlemen. For better or worse, we had at
last arrived on the shores of the New World and perhaps
you will forgive me if I am reminded of a passage from
my novel "Martin Chuzzlewit"...

Lights dim a little.

"And this," said Mr Tapley to Martin Chuzzlewit, looking far ahead, "is the Land of Liberty,
is it? Very well. I'm 'greeable. Any land will do
for me, after so much water!"

Momentary blackout.

Lights come up again, DICKENS still at lectern.

Ladies and gentlemen, how can I tell you what

happened from the first day on shore – give you the faintest conception of my welcome there? If I went out in a carriage, the crowd surrounded it and escorted me home. If I went to the theatre, the whole house (crowded to the roof) would rise as one man, and the timbers would ring again. It is nothing to say that they carried me through the country on their shoulders, or that they flocked about me – "Boz, the Inimitable!" – as if I were an Idol.

Only the newspapers – and this from the start – lent an ear to the sceptical...

(*American accent.*) "Messrs Editors..." (*English accent.*) This to Boston's *Commercial Herald* – (*American accent.*) "Messrs Editors, Have you seen the celebrated Mr Dickens? Well, what do you think of him? The adulation paid him reminds us of European servility, ill-befitting Americans – much less the descendants of the Puritans, who never bowed the knee to any earthly potentate or kissed the toe of any dignitary!"

(*Back to English.*) As for Americans themselves, my first impressions were more than agreeable. They seemed as delicate, as considerate, as careful of giving the least
offence as the best Englishmen I had ever seen. The general breeding was neither stiff nor forward; the
good nature universal. Their ladies are decidedly and unquestionably beautiful... though it was, I discovered, a beauty that soon faded.

Our first visit in a tour intended – I should at once make clear – entirely for our private pleasure was to Boston, where we found our hotel to be only a trifle smaller than Finsbury Square, and made so infernally hot by means of a furnace with pipes running through the passages that we could hardly bear it. But Boston itself? When, wrapped in my fur coat, I first got into the

shining snow-covered streets upon that Sunday morning, the air was so clear; the houses were so bright and
gay; the signboards were painted in such gaudy colours;
the gilded letters, the knobs and plates upon the street
doors were so very golden; the bricks were so very red;
the stone was so very white; the blinds and area railings
were so very green; and all so slight and insubstantial in
appearance – that every thoroughfare in
the city looked exactly like a scene in a pantomime. As
I walked along (or, more truthfully, *ran* along, pulling
the bell-handles of the doors while I went, so marvel-
lously bright and twinkling were they), the whole thing
induced
in me, I confess, one continual shout of uproarious
laughter. Yes indeed! Boston – I thought – is what I
would like the whole United States to be!

At South Boston is the State Hospital for the Insane,
humanely, efficaciously and all in all most admirably
conducted. "This lady," said the resident physician
aloud, taking me by the hand, and advancing to a fantastic figure with great politeness, "This lady is the hostess
of this mansion, sir. It belongs to her." Leaning her head
against the chimney-piece, with a great assumption of
dignity and refinement of manner, sat an elderly female.
Her head in particular was so strewn with scraps of
gauze and cotton and bits of paper, and had so many
queer odds and ends stuck all about it that it looked like
a bird's nest. She was radiant with imaginary jewels and
gracefully dropped upon her lap, as we approached, a
very old greasy newspaper,
in which I dare say she had been reading an account of
her own presentation at some Foreign Court. "She lives,
you observe, in the very first style with a great number
of attendants," continued the physician, not raising her
suspicions by the slightest look or whisper, or any kind
of aside, to me. "She is kind enough to receive my visits,
and to permit my wife and family to reside here; for

which, it is hardly necessary to say, we are much indebted to her. She is exceedingly courteous, you perceive." On this hint she bowed condescendingly and went her way.

Boston harbour I went to see one very fine winter morning: an Italian sky above, and the air so clear and bright on every side that even my eyes, which are none of the best, could follow the minute lines and scraps of tracery in distant buildings. Here stands the Massachusetts Asylum for the Blind, a mile or two without the town,
an airy, spacious, handsome edifice, built upon a height, commanding the harbour. When I paused for a moment at the door, and marked how fresh and free the whole scene was – what sparkling bubbles glanced upon the waves,
and welled up every moment to the surface, as though the world below, like that above, were radiant with the bright day, and gushing over in its fullness of light; when I gazed from sail to sail away upon a ship at sea, a tiny speck of shining white, the only cloud upon the still, deep, distant blue – and, turning, saw a blind boy with his sightless
face addressed that way, as though he too had some sense within him of the glorious distance; I felt a kind of sorrow that the place should be so very light, and a strange wish that for his sake it were darker...

It was in this same harbour but down among the shipping, in one of the narrow, old, water-side streets with
a gay blue flag waving free from its roof, that I heard my only preacher in Boston, one "Mr Taylor", who once had been a mariner himself. He looked a weather-beaten hard-featured man, of about six or eight and fifty, with deep lines graven as it were into his face, dark hair, and a stern keen eye. He opened his discourse, taking for his

text a passage from the Song of Solomon: "Who is this coming up from the wilderness, leaning on the arm of her beloved!" His imagery was all drawn from the sea, and from the incidents of a seaman's life.

"Who are they – who are these fellows? Where do they come from? What's the answer?" – this asked leaning out of the pulpit, and pointing downward with his right hand amid the congregation: "From below, my brethren. From under the hatches of sin, battened down above you by the evil one. That's where you came from!" – a walk up and down the pulpit: "and where are you going" – stopping abruptly: "Aloft!" – very softly, and pointing upward: "Aloft!" – louder; "aloft!" – louder still: "That's where you are going – with a fair wind – all taut and trim, steering direct for Heaven in its glory, where there are no storms or foul weather, and where the wicked cease from troubling, and the weary are at rest." – Another walk: "That's where you're going to, my friends. Leaning upon the arm of the Beloved Saviour – pilot, guiding-star and compass, all in one, to all hands... That's it. That's the place. That's the haven. It's a blessed harbour – still water there, in all changes of the winds and tides; no driving ashore upon the rocks, or slipping your cables and running out to sea, there: Peace – Peace – Peace – all peace!"

Back at my hotel such was the crush to see me I had no choice but to hold daily receptions and take on a secretary. My wife and I were, so to speak, "on duty" from morning until night (my wife, I should add, makes a most admirable traveller in every respect save for her tendency to fall into or out of every coach or boat we enter, scraping the skin off her legs, chipping large fragments out of her ankle-bones and making herself blue with bruises) – we were,

as I say, "on duty" from morning until night and when
I sat for my portrait the staircase and hall of the artist's
studio were filled with people waiting to catch a glimpse
of us. One lady asked, "Mr Dickens, will you be kind
enough to walk entirely round the room, so that we can
all have a look at you?" Some three or four other ladies
solicited a lock of my hair and when I replied I could
not – the precedent would be of a most dangerous and
alarming kind and likely to terminate before long in
my total baldness – word of this travelled ahead of me
to Philadelphia, where, I understand, an advertiser in a
local newspaper, *The Spirit of the Times*, urged me thus:
"Go to it, Boz, don't be selfish, give the ladies a lock of
your hair, and when it is all gone, rub your bald pate
with... Balm of Columbia! to be had at 71 Maiden Lane,
New York, corner of Third and Race, and Muth and
Chestnut Streets, Philadelphia!"

Finally there was to be a public dinner held for me
by certain of Boston's prominent Young Men. It was
the first evening in February, and my first important
public event in America.

The speech I made there was much the same speech
I was to make everywhere in America. In all of them
I returned to the same theme – the absence of international copyright, the piracy of my books, the fact that
neither
I nor any other English writer earned so much as a cent
from any editions in America, where, however, they sold
in their thousands...

I wish you could have seen the faces *I* saw when I
began to talk about Sir Walter Scott. I asked them to
envisage that great man on his last and sad, sad bed,
sinking beneath the mighty pressure on his brain – faint,
wan, dying, knowing that his books were read in his own
tongue in every house and hut of America and yet from

this he derived not one grateful dollar-piece to buy a garland for his grave.

Well, well. This was only the beginning of a sorry story. Some of my more cautious friends felt that I, a man alone by himself in America, should have heeded warnings *not* to suggest that there was one point on which Americans were neither just to their own countrymen nor to us British! One particular newspaper expressed it more pithily: "You must drop that, Charlie, or you will be dished..."

Lights dim a little.

"You have come to visit our country, sir, at a season of great commercial depression," said the Major.

"At an alarming crisis," said the Colonel.

"At a period of unprecedented stagnation," said Mr Jefferson Brick.

"I am sorry to hear that," returned Martin Chuzzlewit. "It's not likely to last, I hope?"

Martin knew nothing about America, or he would have known perfectly well that if its individual citizens, to a man, are to be believed, it always *is* depressed, and always *is* stagnated, and always *is* at an alarming crisis, and never was otherwise; though as a body they are ready to make oath upon the Evangelists at any hour of the day or night, that it is the most thriving and prosperous of all countries on the habitable globe.

"It's not likely to last, I hope?" repeated Martin.

"Well," returned the Major. "I expect we shall get along somehow, and come right in the end."

"We are an elastic country," said the Colonel.

"We are a young lion," said Mr Jefferson Brick.

"We have revivifying and vigorous principles within ourselves!" observed the Major. "Shall we drink a bitter afore dinner, Colonel?"

Momentary blackout.

Lights come up again.

From Boston to Worcester – to Springfield – to Hartford (where I turned thirty) – and then at last New York...

On these occasions I made acquaintance for the first time with the American railroad – which is to say, a great deal of noise, a great deal of wall, not much window, a locomotive engine, a shriek, and a bell.

Everybody talks to you, or to anybody else who hits his fancy. If you are an Englishman, he expects that that railroad is pretty much like an English railroad. If you say "No", he says "Yes?" (interrogatively), and asks in what respect they differ. Then he guesses that you don't travel faster in England, and on your replying that you do, it is quite evident, doesn't believe it. After a long pause he remarks, partly to you, and partly to the knob on the top of his stick, that "Yankees are reckoned to be
a considerable go-ahead people too".

In this part of America the character of the scenery
is always the same. Mile after mile of stunted trees
in every possible stage of decay, decomposition and
neglect until you emerge for a few brief minutes on an
open country glittering with some bright lake or pool,
now catch hasty glimpses of a distant town, with its clean

white houses and their cool piazzas, its prim
New England church and school-house, when whir-r-r-r!
almost before you have seen them, comes the same dark
screen: stumps, logs, stagnant water... The train calls
at stations in the woods where the wild impossibility
of anybody having the smallest reason to get out is only
to be equalled by the apparently desperate hopelessness
of there being anybody to get in. It rushes across the
turnpike road, where there is no gate, no policeman,
no signal; nothing but a rough wooden arch, on which
is painted "WHEN THE BELL RINGS, LOOK OUT
FOR THE LOCOMOTIVE". On it whirls headlong,
drives through the woods again, emerges in the light,
clatters over frail arches, rumbles upon the heavy
ground, shoots beneath a wooden bridge which inter-
cepts the light for a second like a wink, suddenly awak-
ens all the slumbering echoes in the main street
of a large town, and dashes on haphazard, pell-mell,
neck-or-nothing, down the middle of the road. There –
with mechanics working at their trades, and people leaning from their doors and windows, and boys flying kites
and playing marbles, and men smoking, and women
talking, and children crawling, and pigs burrowing, and
unaccustomed horses plunging and rearing, close to the
very rails – there – on, on, on – tears the mad dragon of
an engine with its train of cars; scattering in all directions
a shower of burning sparks from its wood fire; screech-
ing, hissing, yelling, panting; until at last the thirsty monster stops beneath a covered way to drink, the people
cluster round, and you have time to breathe again.

Or rather you don't... For by these twists and turns
you have arrived in the city of New York.

Lights dim a little.

"All men are alike in the U-nited States, an't
they?" said Bill. "It makes no odds whether a man
has a thousand pound, or nothing there. Particular

17

in New York, I'm told, where Ned landed."

"New York, was it?" asked Martin, thoughtfully.

"Yes," said Bill. "New York. I know that, because he sent word home that it brought Old York to his mind, quite vivid, in consequence of being so unlike it in every respect. I don't understand what particular business Ned turned his mind to when he got there... Anyhow, he made his fortune."

"No!" cried Martin.

"Yes, he did," said Bill. "I know that, because he lost it all the day after..."

Momentary blackout.

Lights come up again.

In reality we had come the last stretch to New York City not by train but by steamboat from New Haven. Hence it was across the water that we first caught its life and stir, its hum and buzz. The clinking of capstans, the ringing of bells, the barking of dogs, the cluttering of wheels tingled in the listening ear.

In New York the great promenade and thoroughfare,
as most people know, is Broadway; a wide and bustling street, which, from the Battery Gardens to its opposite termination in a country road, may be four miles long... Shall we sally forth arm-in-arm for a moment, and mingle with the stream?

Warm weather! And was there ever such a sunny street as this Broadway, even in the late afternoon! The pavement stones are polished with the tread of feet until they shine again, and the roofs of those omnibuses look

as though, if water were poured on them, they would
hiss and smoke, and smell like half-quenched fires. Half
a dozen have gone by within as many minutes. Plenty
of hackney cabs and coaches too... Negro coachmen
and white... Some southern republican that, who puts
his blacks in uniform, and swells with Sultan pomp and
power... Heaven save the ladies, how they dress! We
have seen more colours in these last minutes than we
should have seen elsewhere, in as many days. What vari-
ous parasols! what rainbow silks and satins!

But already the evening is closing in, the streets and
shops lighted now, the thoroughfare dotted with bright
jets of gas. And so we turn back towards our hotel taking
care
of the pigs seen roaming towards bed in scores, eating
their way to the last...

Lights dim a little and come back up again.

The great ball – the so-called "Boz-ball" – came off
in New York's Park Theatre on February the fifteenth.
Our carriage took us to the stage door, greatly to the dis-
appointment of an enormous crowd, who were besetting
the main door and making a most tremendous hullabal-
loo.

We walked in through the centre dress-box – the
front
of which had been taken out for the occasion – so to the
back of the stage, where the mayor and other dignitaries
received us, and we were then, for the gratification of
the many-headed who, all in full dress, numbered some
three thousand, paraded twice round what, by covering
the entire pit, had been transformed into an enormous
ball-room. That done, we began to dance – Heaven
knows how we did it,
for there was no room. The walls had been covered in
white muslin and decorated with medallions represent-

ing each
one of my novels interspersed with rosettes and silver
stars, and in the centre a portrait of "Boz" himself! not
sufficiently wary, it seemed to me, of the eagle that hov-
ered above
him with a laurel crown in its beak... Between the different dances a gong sounded, a curtain painted like the
frontispiece of my own *Pickwick Papers* was drawn up
and artists procured for the occasion were discovered
in *tableaux vivants* from my work – to wit, Mrs Bardell
encountering
Mr Pickwick in prison; Mr and Mrs Mantalini in Ralph
Nickleby's office; Oliver Twist at Mrs Maylie's door; Little Nell leading her grandfather... and so on.

We continued dancing, my wife and I, until, about
half past twelve o'clock, being no longer able even to
stand, we slipped away quietly and came back to the
hotel.

After the ball I was laid up with a very bad sore
throat. That my wife was also ill led me to speculate if
it be not the fault of the American heating-system... For
four whole days
I was confined to the hotel, unable to write or indeed
to do anything but doze, drink lemonade and read the
newspapers.

Was it *then* I began to feel dispirited, sick to death
of the life I had been leading and sad with thoughts of
home? – and this less than half-way through our visit!

On the subject of International Copyright – of which,
you will remember, I had spoken at Boston and again at
Hartford – it seems no sooner had I made these speeches
than an outcry began as an Englishman can form no notion of. Would I have had so many readers, I was asked, if
it had not been
for these cheap reprints? Besides – my novels were read

and liked by all Americans; here was reward enough for
any man! What *more* would I have?... Now, it seemed,
it was war to the knife. Assertions that I was "no gentleman", but "a mere mercenary scoundrel". Attacks and
verbal dissuasions by
the score came pouring in upon me every day.

The American people are warm-hearted, fervent, and
enthusiastic, full of the most affectionate and generous
impulses. But "freedom of opinion"? Where is it? I see
a press more mean and paltry and silly and disgraceful
than
in any country I ever knew. I declare I began to tremble
for any radical coming here. As for myself I believe in
the United States I should have lived and died poor, un-
noticed and a black sheep.

... And now even the fêting and feasting left me only
weary and distressed. I could do nothing that I wanted
to
do, go nowhere where I wanted to go and see nothing
that
I wanted to see. So it was I resolved for the future to
shake hands with Americans not at parties but at home.

Lights dim a little.

"How do you like our country, Sir?" Chollop
inquired, looking at Martin.

"Not at all," was his reply.

"I am not surprised to hear you say so. It
re-quires An Elevation, and A Preparation of the
intellect. The mind of man must be prepared for
Freedom, Mister!"

Momentary blackout.

Lights come up again.

The journey from New York to Philadelphia is made by railroad and two ferries, and usually occupies between five and six hours.

It was a fine evening when we were passengers in the train, and, watching the bright sunset from a little window near the door by which we sat, my attention was attracted to a remarkable appearance issuing from the windows
of the gentleman's car immediately in front of us, which I supposed for some time was occasioned by a number of industrious persons inside, ripping open feather beds, and giving the feathers to the wind. At length it occurred to me that these were flashes of saliva, flying perpetually and incessantly, and that the men in the car ahead of us were spitting... a practice which seems universal here: in the stage-coach, the steam-boat, in the hospital, the hall of a private gentleman, and in the chamber of Congress. In every bar-room and hotel passage, on the marble stairs and passages of every handsome public building, the stone floor looks as if it were paved with open oysters from the quantity of this kind of deposit... I believe I would be content even to live in an atmosphere of spit, if they would but *spit clean*, but when every man ejects from his mouth that odious, most disgusting brown compound of saliva and tobacco – their quids, or "plugs" as I have heard them called – I vow that my stomach revolts, and I cannot endure it!

Our stay in Philadelphia was very short. It proved a handsome city... but distractingly regular. After walking about it for an hour or two, I felt that I would have given the world for a crooked street. Beneath its quakery influence my coat appeared to stiffen and the brim of my hat to expand. My hair shrank in a sleek short crop, my hands folded themselves upon my breast of their own calm accord, and thoughts came over me involuntarily of making a large fortune by speculation in corn.

In the outskirts stands a great prison called the
Eastern Penitentiary, conducted on a famous plan – the
Separate System – peculiar to the state of Pennsylvania
and based
on the belief that reformation of prisoners is only possible
if they be separated from criminal companions.

I spent a whole day here, going from cell to cell...

Over the head and face of every prisoner who comes
into this melancholy house – he comes, by the way,
always at night – a black hood is drawn, and in this dark
shroud,
an emblem of the curtain dropped between him and the
living world, he is led to the cell from which he never
again comes forth, until his whole term of imprisonment
has expired. He never hears of wife and children, home
or friends, the life and death of any single creature. He
sees the prison officers, but with that exception he never
looks upon a human countenance or hears a human
voice. He is a man buried alive, to be dug out in the
slow round of the years, and in the meantime dead to
everything but torturing anxieties and horrible despair...
One man had been shut up by himself in the same cell
for nearly twelve years. His time was just expiring. I
asked him how he felt at the prospect of release, and he
answered – plucking in a strange way at his fingers, and
looking restlessly about the walls and floors – that he
didn't care; that it was all the same to him now; that he
had looked forward to it once, but that was so long ago,
that he had come to have no regard for anything. And
so, with a heavy sigh, he went about his work – largely
weaving and shoe-making – and would say no more.

What else should one expect? Better, I say, to have
hanged him in the beginning than bring him to this pass,
and send him forth to mingle with his kind who are his
kind no more!

Lights dim a little and come back up again.

In Washington one "Mr Tyler", President of the United States, sat all alone by the side of a hot stove, though it
was a very hot day, this mid-March, with the Spring fever coming on, and where, it seems, the thermometer is frequently taking a little trip of thirty degrees between sunrise and sunset. Close to him was his great spit-box, the indispensable article of furniture here in a city which is the headquarters of tobacco-tinctured saliva. Indeed down below, waiting for audience in another room, were some twenty gentlemen expectorating considerably and wreaking a complete change in the pattern of the carpet.

The President got up and said, "Is *this* Mr Dickens?"

"Sir", returned Mr Dickens, "it is."

"I am astonished to see so young a man, Sir," said the President.

Mr Dickens smiled, and thought of returning the compliment – but he didn't, for the President looked too worn and tired to justify it.

"I am happy to join with my fellow citizens in welcoming you, warmly, to this country," said the President.

Mr Dickens thanked him and shook hands. Then the other Mr Dickens – I should explain that the Secretary to the Senate bore, confusingly, the same name as myself – asked the President to come to his house that night, which the President said he should be glad to do but for the pressure of business, and measles. And, the English Mr Dickens and the American Mr Dickens going their separate ways, that was the end of the conference.

... And so – with the "City of Magnificent Intentions" behind us (for thus Washington might be termed

with its spacious avenues beginning in nothing and leading
nowhere, with no trade or commerce of its own and
with little or no population beyond the President, the
legislature and the hotel-keepers and tradesmen who
supply their tables) – with Washington, I say, behind
us – we could leave the last of these big cities and finally
begin to travel, for the railroad distances we had so far
traversed in journeying among these older towns are on
that great continent looked upon as nothing. I began to
listen to old whisperings which had often been present
to me at home in England, when I little thought of ever
being here, and to dream again of cities growing up like
palaces in fairy tales, among the wilds and forests of the
west...

Now we passed through regions of spittoons, senators
and slavery, and the sensation of exacting any service
from human creatures who are bought and sold, and
being for the time a party as it were to their condition,
filled me with a sense of shame and self-reproach...

Leaving Baltimore in the morning by railroad, we
got to a place called York, where we dined about twelve
and took a stagecoach for Harrisburg, twenty-five miles
further.

This stagecoach was like nothing so much as the body
of one of the swings you see at a fair set upon four
wheels and roofed and covered at the sides with painted canvas. There were *twelve* inside! Despite the rain
I, thank my stars, was on the box, beside as it happens
what I took to be a rather large fiddle in a brown bag.
In the course of ten
miles or so, however, I discovered that it had a pair of
dirty shoes at one end, and a glazed cap at the other,
and further observation demonstrated it to be a small

boy, in
a snuff-coloured coat, with his arms quite pinioned to
his sides by a deep forcing into his pockets. When we
stopped to water the horses, about two miles from Harrisburg,
this thing that had apparently slept all the way, its face
to the wind, slowly upreared itself to the height of three
foot eight, and fixing its eyes on me with a mingled expression of complacency, patronage, national independ-
ence, and sympathy for all outer barbarians
and foreigners, said, in shrill piping accents, "Well now,
stranger, I guess you find this, a'most like an English
a'ternoon – hey?"

It is unnecessary to add that I thirsted for his blood...

And now to Pittsburgh – some 350 miles due West –
by the Main Line Canal, where you might have seen
me
in the morning between five and six, jumping from the
boat to the towing-path and walking six or seven miles
before breakfast, keeping up with the horses all the
time, and the other good people on board quite astonished to find a sedentary Englishman roughing it so well
and taking so much exercise.

Exquisite weather, this late March of 42, but cold
again: clear starlight and moonlit nights, the canal running for the most part by the side of the Susquehanah
and Iwanata rivers, often through deep, sullen gorges
and only the crossing of the Alleghany Mountains to be
done by railroad – a rapid pace, a keen wind, looking
down into a valley full of light and softness, catching
glimpses through the treetops of scattered cabins, children running to the doors, dogs bursting out to bark,
terrified pigs scampering homewards, families sitting out
in their gardens, cows gazing up with
a stupid indifference, men in their shirt-sleeves looking

on
at their unfinished houses, planning out tomorrow's
work...
and we riding onward, high above them, like a whirl-
wind. *This* was beautiful – very, very beautiful!

Thus we travelled to Pittsburgh, a town much like
Birmingham in England. At least its townsfolk say so.
Setting aside the streets, the shops, houses, wagons,
factories, public buildings and population – I suppose
it is. At least in respect of a great deal of smoke, and its
iron-works...

Here we tarried three days before taking a steamboat
for Cincinnati – only fifty years old, but a very beautiful
city – I think the prettiest place I had seen except Boston
– risen out of the forest like an Arabian-night city.

I have referred already to my wife's propensity for
accident (once – towards the end of our travels – she was
lying in a languishing manner with her neck upon the
open window when our stage-coach went over a road
made of tree-trunks thrown into a marsh... Bump! Crash!
She very nearly had her head taken off and to this hour
it is a little
on one side) – but I have said nothing of the reactions of
her maid Anne. The reason is simple. I don't think that
in the whole six months of our travels she so much as
saw
an American tree. She never looked at a prospect by any
chance or displayed the smallest emotion at any sight
whatever. Here in Cincinnati, at least, she was obliged
so to do: as we made our way on foot over the broken
pavement, she measured her length upon the ground
but didn't hurt herself... My wife – who is always most
perfectly game –
has done likewise a mere three hundred and forty times.

... And so we moved on, this time by riverboat. "The

great Mississippi"? Bah! An enormous ditch, sometimes
two or three miles wide, running liquid mud, its strong
and frothy current choked and obstructed everywhere
by huge logs and whole forest trees. The banks low, the
trees dwarfish, the marshes swarming with frogs, the
wretched cabins few and far apart, their inmates hollow-
cheeked
and pale, the weather very hot, mosquitoes penetrating
into every crack and crevice of the boat, mud and slime
on everything. Only the decline of the day here was
very gorgeous, tingeing the firmament deeply with red
and gold, up to the very keystone of the arch above us.

We had a very crowded reception in St Louis. Their
paper had an account of it (if I had dropped a letter in the
street
I believe it would have been in the newspaper the next
day) – the editor objecting to my hair as not curling sufficiently and to my dress as being somewhat "foppish" not
to say "flash"... "But such," he benevolently added, "are
the differences between American and English taste."
In the same spirit a lady of St Louis complimented my
wife upon her voice and manner of speaking, assuring
her that she should never have suspected her of being
Scotch or even English, adding she would have taken
her for an American anywhere – and
no doubt my wife was aware that this was a very great
compliment as the Americans were admitted on all
hands
to have greatly refined upon the English language.

Lights dim a little.

"I have always remarked it as a very extraordinary circumstance," said General Choke, holding
up his hand, "that the knowledge of Britishers
themselves on points of English life is not to be
compared with that possessed by our intelligent

and locomotive citizens..."

"When you say, Sir," he continued, addressing Martin, "that your Queen does not reside in the Tower of London, you fall into an error not uncommon to your countrymen... Sir, you are wrong. She *does* live there. For if her location was in Windsor Pavilion it couldn't be in London at the same time. Your Tower of London, Sir," pursued the General, smiling with a mild consciousness of this knowledge, "is nat'rally your royal residence. Being located in the immediate neighbourhood of your Parks, your Drives, your Triumphant Arches, your Opera, and your Royal Almacks, it nat'rally suggests itself as the place for holding a luxurious and thoughtless court. And, consequently," said the General, "consequently, the court is held there."

"Have you been in England?" asked Martin.

"In print I have, sir," said the General, "not otherwise. We are a reading people here, sir. You will meet with much information among us that will surprise you, sir."

"I have not the least doubt of it," returned Martin.

"The Queen of England, gentlemen," added Mark, affecting the greatest politeness and regarding these Americans with an immovable face, "The Queen of England usually lives in the Mint to take care of the money. She has lodgings, in virtue of her office, with the Lord Mayor at the Mansion-House, but don't often occupy them, in consequence of the parlour chimney smoking..."

Momentary blackout.

Lights come up again.

The Looking-Glass Prairie is within thirty miles of
St Louis and we got upon it at sunset. It is widely-famed,
but I would say to every man who can't see a prairie –
go to Salisbury plain, Marlborough downs, or any of our
broad, high, open lands near the sea. Many of them are
fully as impressive, and Salisbury plain is decidedly *more*
so!

But coming on by railroad from Buffalo next day –
and nigh two hours upon the way – I never in my life
was
in such a state of excitement. I looked out for the spray
and listened for the roar of the Niagara Falls far beyond the bounds of possibility. At last, when the train
stopped,
I saw two great white clouds rising up from the depths of
the earth – nothing more. They rose up slowly, gently,
majestically, into the air. I dragged Kate down a deep
and slippery path leading to the ferry boat, bullied Anne
the maid for not coming fast enough, perspired at every
pore, and felt it is impossible to say how as the sound
grew louder and louder in my ears and yet nothing
could be seen for the mist.

Clambering over the rocks, blinded by the spray and
wet to the skin, I went down alone, into the very basin...

It would be hard for a man to stand nearer to God
than he does there. There was a bright rainbow at my
feet, and from that I looked up – great Heaven! to *what*
a fall of bright green water! The broad, deep, mighty
stream seems to die in the act of falling, and from its
unfathomable grave arises that tremendous ghost of
spray and mist which is never laid, and has been haunt-
ing this place with the same dread solemnity – perhaps
from the creation of the world. The first effect and the
enduring one – instant and lasting – of the tremendous

spectacle was Peace. Peace of Mind, tranquillity, calm recollections of the Dead, great thoughts of Eternal rest and Happiness, nothing of gloom or terror. Niagara was at once stamped upon my heart, an Image of Beauty; to remain there, changeless and indelible, until its pulses cease to beat for ever...

When, later, I asked our maid Anne what she made of Niagara she remained true to her character. "Why, Sir! –
it's nothing but water... And much too much of that!"

Lights dim a little and come back up again.

To be sure, there were other last journeys – through the rich and beautiful Kaatskill mountains – to a Shaker village arriving to find ourselves in a grim room, where several grim hats were hanging on grim pegs, and the time was told by a grim clock which uttered every tick with a kind of struggle, as if it broke the grim silence reluctantly, and under protest. On, briefly, to Montreal... and back to New York.

From the heights of the Alleghany Mountains, from the surface of the Lakes we traversed, amidst the silence of the broad prairies we crossed, and high above the roar and spray of dread Niagara... we had travelled so far and
so constantly by land and water, by coach and steamer, by wagon and railway, that by the time we reached home
we had travelled ten thousand miles or more.

I had not changed my secret opinion of this country; its follies, vices, grievous disappointments. I believed the heaviest blow ever dealt at Liberty's Head would be dealt
by this nation in the ultimate failure of its example to the Earth. The exhausted Treasury; the paralysed govern-

ment; the silly, drivelling, slanderous, wicked, monstrous Party Press... In brief, I decided I hadn't liked it. It went against the grain with me. I would not live there on any consideration and concluded it was impossible, utterly impossible for *any* Englishman to live there and be happy.

I say all this, and yet I had come to love and honour very many of the people. Among all the thousands whom
I had seen, within doors and without (and they were so many that I almost paralysed my right arm by constantly shaking hands), I had never once encountered a man, woman, or child, who asked me a rude question or made a rude remark. I had not travelled anywhere, without making upon the road a pleasant acquaintance who had gone out of his way to serve and assist me. They were as a people generous, hospitable, affectionate, and kind.

... We left America. The places we had lodged in; the roads we had gone over; the tobacco spittle we had wallowed in – all this and the company we had been among became subjects for legend and tales at home. In *my* case, subject for
a novel "Martin Chuzzlewit" – in which I was unwise enough to voice, albeit comically, many of my reservations.

Lights dim a little.

"But where?" cried Tom. "Oh where will you go?"

"I don't know," Martin said. "Yes. I do. I'll go to America!"

"No, no," cried Tom, in a kind of agony. "Pray don't go there. Think better of it. Don't go to America! Don't be so dreadfully regardless of yourself!"

Lights come up again.

My gentle listeners will not, perhaps, be surprised to learn that it was another twenty-five years before I was invited to return...

Lights dim. He smiles, bows quickly and leaves the stage.

Blackout.

End of Part One.

PART TWO

Lights come up. DICKENS is already at his lectern, some twenty-five years older than in the first part.

He is now fifty-six. With his grizzled beard, thinning hair and deeply lined face, he could pass for a man in his sixties. And yet – despite having less than three years left to live – he is still dapper to the point of "flash", and has lost neither his brilliance of eye nor his quick-changing facial expression.

We discover him in medias res.

Paul had never risen from his little bed. He lay there, listening to the noises in the street, quite tranquilly; not caring much how the time went, but watching it and watching everything about him with observing eyes.

When the sunbeams struck into his room through the rustling blinds, and quivered on the opposite wall like golden water, he knew that evening was coming on, and that the sky was red and beautiful. As the reflection died away, and a gloom went creeping up the wall, he watched it deepen, deepen, deepen, into night. Then he thought how the long streets were dotted with lamps, and how the peaceful stars were shining overhead. His fancy had a strange tendency to wander to the river, which he knew was flowing through the great city; and now he thought how black it was, and how deep it would look, reflecting the hosts of stars – and more than all, how steadily it rolled away to meet the sea...

Sister and brother wound their arms around each other, and the golden light came streaming in, and fell upon them, locked together.

"How fast the river runs, between its green banks

and the rushes, Floy! But it's very near the sea. I hear the waves! They always said so!"

Presently he told her that the motion of the boat upon the stream was lulling him to rest. How green the banks were now, how bright the flowers growing on them, and how tall the rushes! Now the boat was out at sea, but gliding smoothly on.

The golden ripple on the wall came back again, and nothing else stirred in the room. The old, old fashion! The fashion that came in with our first garments, and will last unchanged until our race has run its course, and the wide firmament is rolled up like a scroll. The old, old fashion – Death!

Oh thank God, all who see it, for that older fashion yet, of Immortality! And look upon us, angels of young children, with regards not quite estranged, when the swift river bears us to the ocean!

Off, great applause.

Lights dim a little... and come up again.

Now more directly to the audience:

Once again – and some twenty-five years later – an ocean called the Atlantic had borne me back to America, where from November 1867 until April of 1868 I had agreed to give a series of public readings from my novels, the story of little Paul Dombey and his death being just one of them...

This was to be work – hard work – profitable, yes, but by no means a visit merely for pleasure to certain major cities of America, as it had been that time before, when

I had come with a wife I now no longer saw, a vitality of health I no longer knew, and when the present much-missed companion of my life (obliged, alas, to stay in England) had been, I calculate, a mere three years old.

I arrived on Tuesday, 19 November, in Boston – my first stop – taking up residence at the Parker House Hotel, where I had stayed twenty-five years earlier... My journey out on the ship *Cuba* had seen some heavy gales, but in my case no sea-sickness, thanks to the admirable preventive of baked apples!

Just as Boston itself seemed to have increased pro-digiously, growing more mercantile – a little (if you will) like Leeds mixed with Preston, and flavoured with New Brighton, only instead of smoke and fog, an exquisitely bright little air – so my hotel, which formerly I had thought a big one, was now regarded as a very small affair. Here I was to live very high up, and had a hot and cold bath in my bedroom, with other comforts not in existence in my former day. Indeed there seemed more of New York in this fine city than there had been of yore and the cost of living was *enormous*. What cared I? Still I received not one cent for books of mine pub-lished or dramatised here (all of these without my per-mission), but tickets for my first four readings in Boston had all been sold immediately they were made available. An immense train of people, I learned, had waited in the freezing street for twelve hours.

As for the old grudges and rancour (would they forgive me, I wondered, for my strictures in "Martin Chuzzlewit" and "American Notes"?) all seemed to be forgotten: the greeting was full as extraordinary as that of twenty-five years earlier. One Boston newspaper went so far as to claim that all the streets of the city had

been swept twice over with a view to my coming and
that the State hall and the Old South Church had been
painted anew – this time
a delicate rose pink.

I had arrived with a travelling staff of five includ-
ing Scott, my dresser and new valet, and Kelly, a
general factotum. Representative of Mr James Fields,
my American publisher, and travelling with us, would
be a Mr Osgood. Also brought over from England as
manager for my tour was Mr George Dolby – soon to
become the most unpopular and best-abused fellow in
America for
his inability to get 4,000 people into a room holding
only 2,000, likewise his failure to induce people to pay at
the ordinary price for themselves instead of giving
thrice as much to speculators in our tickets. Ah – the
"speculators"! More of them anon!

For my first reading in Boston I took *A Christmas
Carol* and The Trial from *Pickwick's Papers*. The next day,
it seemed, the whole city would talk of nothing else, and
hear of nothing else. Dolby claimed that the queue for
tickets was now so wild as to suggest the night before an
execution at the Old Bailey.

"Tain't election-time down here, is it?"
"Oh no, we're buying tickets, Sir."
"Buying tickets?... for what?"
"For Dickens's Readings."
"Dickens! Who the devil is Dickens?"
"Why, don't you know? The great novelist!...
    You must be from outa town!"

The booksellers' windows all filled with my novels
and now, in other kinds of shop, you could buy a "Little
Nell Cigar" or some "Pickwick Snuff".

Resting only on the Wednesday night I read again

every evening of that week, making a clear profit of thirteen hundred pounds, and travelled to New York on the Saturday, aware only dimly that the weather was taking a turn of unusual severity...

And New York itself? Amazing success! A very fine audience, far better even than at Boston – in its appreciation quick and unfailing, in its satisfactions highly demonstrative. "Mr Digguns," said the German janitor or hall-keeper of my hotel, "you are gread, mein herr. There is no ent to you!" This would be his parting salutation to me each morning as he pushed me out into a hard frost... "Bedder and bedder", he re-opened the door to add, "Wot negst?!"

In the queues, members of families relieved each other; waiters flew across the streets and squares from the neighbouring restaurant, to serve parties who were taking their breakfast in the open December air; while excited
men offered five and ten dollars for the mere permission to exchange places with other persons standing nearer the head of the line... No sooner had I arrived in the city myself than I was receiving letters from persons who were all apparently blind, crippled or paralysed, and thus unable to join a queue. Such were the numbers one man thought the occasion – and presumably his own need of a ticket – warranted an oration. It began, "Gentlemen, there are but three men who have stamped themselves upon the civilization of the nineteenth century. Those men are Charles Shakespeare, William Dickens – and myself."... Well, well. It had occurred to me before that Americans must not have a thing too easily. Nothing in the country lasts long, and a thing is prized the more, the less easy it is made: the tickets for the course were all sold before noon.

... Thus, for over two months, I journeyed back and

forth between New York and Boston. The press for tickets
continued such that my manager Dolby, already the most
unpopular
of men, was reviled in print daily. Typical was one
morning newspaper: "Surely it is time that the pudding-
headed Dolby retired into the native gloom from which
he has emerged."
In consequence Scott, Osgood and I started now to call
him "P.H." Dolby – in homage to his "pudding-headed"
nature – and derived much entertainment from the in-
creasingly fantastic, and totally mendacious, adventures
attributed to him in the American press, *exempli gratia*:
"The chap calling himself Dolby got drunk last night
down town and was locked up in the police station for
fighting an Irishman..."

The people of Boston were in all other respects perfectly kind and perfectly agreeable; people would turn
back, turn again and face me, and have a look at me or
would say to one another, "Look here! Dickens coming!", and certainly
if I stopped to look in at a shop-window a score of
passers-by would also stop... But every day I took a walk
from seven to ten miles in peace.

Likewise in New York – a city, by the way, it took
me
a week to identify as that which I had known a quarter
of
a century before, so prodigiously had it changed. Here
Dolby had happily made up his mind that the less
I was exhibited for nothing the better, and though I
could not
get down Broadway for my own portrait, though all
over
the city they seemed every night to be doing versions
of *Oliver Twist* or *Cricket on the Hearth* or *Our Mutual
Friend,*

and I don't know what else, (needless to say, with no remuneration for myself...) up in my hotel I could come and go by a private door and a private staircase communicating with my bedroom, living as quietly as if I were at the office, with a servant seated outside my public door to wrestle with mankind. I took breakfast in my sitting room, rehearsed there for the evening, took a light lunch and my long walk, finally arriving at the theatre in good time for my reading... Thus I lived my American life.

I don't think that a single night passed in all the time I was in New York without my hearing the fire-bells dolefully clanging all over the city.

One night I was getting into bed just at twelve o'clock, when Dolby came to my door to inform me that our own hotel was on fire. I got Scott up directly; told him first to pack the books and clothes for the readings; dressed, and pocketed my jewels and papers; while Dolby stuffed himself out with money. Meanwhile the police and firemen were in the house tracing the mischief to its source in a certain fire-grate. By this time the hose was laid all through from a great tank on the roof, and everybody turned out to help. It was the oddest sight, and people had put the strangest things on with their most precious possessions under their arms or imperfectly crammed into their pockets! After chopping and cutting with axes through stairs, and much handing about of water, the fire was confined to a dining-room in which it had originated, and then everybody talked to everybody else, the ladies being particularly loquacious and cheerful. I may remark that the landlord no sooner saw me on this agitating occasion – we all eventually got to bed again about two – than, with his property blazing, he insisted on taking me down into a room full of hot smoke, to

drink with him a combination of brandy, water and
snow which he called a "Rocky Mountain Sneezer" –
not of course to be confused with the favourite drink you
get up with, known as an
"Eye-Opener". This drink of his – mixed also with bit-
ters, lemon and sugar – can only be made in its "true"
form,
he maintained, when snow is lying on the ground.

As indeed it was...

When the first snow fell, the railways were closed
for some days. Picture in consequence a New York now
crowded with sleighs – in the park that Sunday there
were at least one thousand of them – and the snow piled
up in enormous walls the whole length of the streets. For
my
part I turned out in a rather gorgeous red sleigh with
any quantity of buffalo robes, drawn by a pair of fine
horses covered with bells and tearing up fourteen miles
of snow an hour. I made an imposing appearance: if you
had beheld me driving out, furred up to the moustache,
with an immense white red-and-yellow striped rug for a
covering, you would have supposed me of Hungarian or
Polish nationality.

But these protections of mine were to no avail. When
the time came for getting back to Boston I had begun to
develop a fearsome cold in the head. In the week before
Christmas this, combined with the low action of the heart
(or whatever
it was), inconvenienced me greatly and after the Mon-
day evening reading I was laid upon the bed, in a very
faint and shaky state. The next day I did not get up till
the afternoon.

America is a bad country to be unwell and travelling
in – this, my "true American catarrh", was infallibly

brought back by every railway car I entered thereafter
owing to their infernal heating – and my dismal cold arrived good and proper on Christmas morning itself.
It was not to be thrown off during my whole stay, and it
seemed my only safe course was to hold to the principle
I had earlier established: gloomily deny myself all grand
public dinners, avoid much travelling or visiting and try
to get the people to come to me, instead of me going
to them. I am bound to disclaim the least merit in this
virtuous-looking self-denial: I retired to the cloister –
my bed and my dreams – as discontentedly and growl-
ingly as possible...

Lights dim a little.

The Spirit stood among the graves, and
pointed down to one...

"Before I draw near to that stone to which you
point," said Scrooge, "answer me one question.
Are these the shadows of things that Will be, or
are they shadows of things that May be, only?"

Still the Ghost was as immovable as ever.

Scrooge crept towards it, trembling as he
went; and following the finger, read upon the
stone of the neglected grave his own name,
EBENEZER SCROOGE.

"No, Spirit! Oh, no no!"

The finger still was there.

"Spirit!" he cried, tight clutching at its robe, "hear
me! I am not the man I was. I will not be the man
I must have been but for this intercourse. Why
show me this, if I am past all hope!"

For the first time the hand appeared to shake.

"Good Spirit," he pursued, as down upon the ground he fell before it: "Your nature intercedes for me, and pities me. Assure me that I yet may change these shadows you have shown me, by an altered life!"

The kind hand trembled.

"I will honour Christmas in my heart, and try to keep it all the year. I will live in the Past, the Present, and the Future. The Spirits of all Three shall strive within me..."

Long pause. Light change.

Scrooge was better than his word. He did it all, and infinitely more. He became as good a friend, as good a master, and as good a man, as the good old city knew, or any other good old city, town, or borough, in the good old world. Some people laughed to see the alteration in him, but he let them laugh, and little heeded them... His own heart laughed; and that was quite enough for him.

Momentary blackout.

Lights come up again.

Two days after Christmas – Christmas Day itself spent travelling back to New York, where I was to read on the 26th, and beginning to suffer from the most acute depression – I was now so very unwell I sent for a doctor, who expressed doubt whether I should not have to stop reading for a while until I pointed out to him how we stood committed. And now – to make matters worse – my next train journey between Boston and New York proved truly alarming...

Two rivers had to be crossed, and each time the whole train was banged aboard a big steamer. The steamer rose and fell with the river, and the train up or down with it.

In coming off the steamer at one of these crossings, we were banged up such a height that the rope broke, and one carriage rushed back with a run downhill into the boat again. I whisked out in a moment, and two or three after me, but nobody else seemed to care about it. I beheld Scott, my valet, leaning a flushed countenance against the side of the carriage and weeping bitterly. I asked him what was the matter, and he replied: "The owdacious treatment of the luggage, which is more outrageous than a man can bear." My writing-desk was smashed and I think every trunk we had was broken... I told him not to make a fool
of himself.

Meanwhile, Dolby was always going about with an immense bundle that looked like a sofa-cushion, but was in reality paper-money. By the time he left briefly for Philadelphia – going ahead to verify all was ar-ranged
as we should wish for the readings there – this had risen to the proportions of a sofa pure and simple...

Well, the work was hard, the climate hard and the life hard, but already the gain was enormous... Philadelphia. Six nights altogether. All tickets long sold... Here I lodged at the Continental, found the town very clean and the days as blue and bright as any fine Italian day; cold and frosty without snow – the best weather for me. According to their newspapers, the Philadelphia audi-ence took "Mr Dickens's extraordinary composure" – their great phrase – rather ill and on the whole implied that it would have been taken as
a suitable compliment if I had staggered on to the plat-form and instantly dropped to the floor, overpowered by the spectacle before me each night instead of simply walking
in and opening my book to read without flourish as I did. Those same newspapers informed the city that "Mr Dickens is not like the descriptions we have read of him

at the little red desk. He is not foppish in appearance at
all. He wears
a heavy moustache and a Vandyke beard and looks...
like
a well-to-do Philadelphia gentleman"!

And so for the present we came back to New York
and Brooklyn, which – you must understand – is a kind
of sleeping-place for New York.

Already the sale of tickets there had been an amazing scene. The noble army of speculators were now
furnished each man with a straw mattress, a little bag of
bread and meat, two blankets and a bottle of whiskey.
With this outfit, they would lie down in line on the pavement the whole of the night before the tickets were sold,
generally taking
up their position at about 10. It being severely cold at
Brooklyn, they made an immense bonfire in the street –
a narrow street of wooden houses – which the police
turned out to extinguish. A general fight then took place;
from which the people farthest off in the line rushed
bleeding when they saw any chance of ousting others
nearer the door, put their mattresses in the spots so
gained, and held on by the iron rails. At 8 in the morning Dolby appeared with the tickets in a portmanteau...
and concluded (as usual) by giving universal dissatisfac-
tion.

During all this time, the men in my team worked
very hard, with only few opportunities for recreation.
One night in New York my valet Scott (with a portmanteau across his knees and a wide-awake hat low down
upon his nose) told me that he had presented himself for
admission at the circus and had been refused.

"The only theayter," he said in a melancholy way,
"as I was ever in my life turned from the door of."

Says Kelly – another member of our crew, you'll

recall: "There must have been some mistake, Scott, because George and me went, and we said, 'Mr Dickens's staff', and they passed us to the best seats in the house. Go again, Scott."

"No, I thank you, Kelly," says Scott, more melancholy than before, "I'm not a-going to put myself in the position of being refused again. It's the only theayter as I was ever turned from the doors of, and it shan't be done twice. But
it's a beastly country!"

"Scott," interposed Mr Lowndes – a third, "don't you express your opinions 'bout the country."

"No, sir," says Scott," I never do, please, sir, but when you are turned from the door of the only theayter you was ever turned from, sir, and when the beasts in railway cars spits tobacco over your boots, you (*privately*) find yourself
in a *beastly* country!"

And my health in this? My cold steadily refused to stir an inch, though it was always good enough to leave me
for the needful two hours of the readings. I tried allopathy, homeopathy, cold things, warm things, sweet things, bitter things, stimulants, narcotics, all with the same result. Nothing would touch it.

Well, well. I was not so foolish as to suppose that all my work could have been achieved without *some* penalty; I had noticed for some time a decided change in my buoyancy and hopefulness – in other words, in my usual 'tone'– only too happy to retire to my hotel, where – on occasion – seated by the fireside, in the solitude of my own room, I would find myself overtaken by a sudden access of melancholy...

Why was I here? Heaven knows, that sad early time

of my life, when I had felt myself beyond the reach of all honourable emulation and success, was now thankfully long past. Here in America we were doing enormous business and the prize was large. More even than my effort to be financially secure, here – waiting to be made – was a *fortune*! here was *triumph*!

That income denied me through the piracy of my books? Those critics and enemies who had attacked me in the American newspapers twenty-five years before? These would be answered and accounted for with interest!

... And yet, and yet. Ever and anon I would find my thoughts tending towards Home, my spirits fluttering woefully towards one certain place, a person most drearily missed – my beloved, my darling, my own dear Nelly...

For a moment he is painfully "elsewhere". Finally "coming round":

In consequence of all this, Dolby and Osgood – who would do the most ridiculous things to keep me in spirits – decided to plan (a good way ahead) a walking-match, this to be at Boston on Saturday, February 29th.

Much to Osgood's terror, Dolby at once sent home for a pair of seamless socks to walk in while Scott and others of our retinue started to become hugely excited on the subject, already and continually making bets on "their man". I and my publisher Fields were to walk out six miles with Osgood and Dolby beside us, until, ourselves reaching the limit, *they* would turn and walk back again.

Neither of them had the least notion what twelve miles at a pace was, and would have the absurdest ideas of what were tests of walking power – as the days passed, they would continually get up in the

maddest manner and
see *how high they could kick the wall*! To see them doing
this – Dolby a big man and Osgood a very little one
– was ridiculous beyond belief, the wainscot in our
hotel becoming scored all over with their competi-
tive pencil-marks... More of this anon! I for my part
started going out in a sleigh and four with inconceivable
dignity
and grandeur!

We were now entered into February and on the first
day of that month I travelled down to Washington for
my readings there... We were not a bit too soon, for the
whole country was beginning to be stirred and shaken
by the presidential election. One evening I was reading
from
A Christmas Carol – "'Hallo!' growled Scrooge in his ac-
customed voice.'What do you mean by coming here at
this time of day?' 'I am very sorry, sir,' said Bob, 'I *am*
behind my time'" – when all of a sudden I saw a dog
leap out from among the seats in the centre aisle and
look very intently at me. I don't think anybody else
saw this dog,
but when he bounced out into the centre aisle again, in
an entirely new place, and (still looking intently at me)
tried the effect of a bark upon the proceedings, I was
seized
with such a paroxysm of laughter that it communicated
itself to the audience, and we roared at one another,
loud and long. Next night I was reading from *Copperfield*
when
I thought I heard a suddenly-suppressed bark. It had
happened in this way: Osgood – it seemed – standing
just within the door, felt his leg touched, and looking
down beheld the dog, staring intently at me, and evidently just about to bark. In a transport of mind and
fury, he instantly caught him up in both hands, and

threw him over his own head out into the entry, where the
check-takers received him like
a game at ball. The following and last night, nothing
discouraged, he came again! – *with another dog*; but our
people were so sharply on the look-out for him that he
wasn't allowed in. He had evidently promised to get
the other dog in, free...

Against my own rules, I accepted an invitation
to dinner in Washington, with Charles Sumner – an
American senator and an old friend. Also there was
Mr Secretary Stanton – Minister of War. He had been
commander-in-chief of all the Northern forces concentrated there and reputedly never went to sleep at night
without first reading something from my books, which
were always with him.
I put him through a pretty severe examination, but he
was better up on them than I was. He and Sumner had
been the first two public men at the bedside of President
Abraham Lincoln when he died, and he went on to tell
me a curious little story...

One afternoon, there was a cabinet council at which
Lincoln presided. Mr Stanton, being – as I have said –
commander-in-chief of the Northern troops that were
concentrated about there, arrived rather late and found
President Lincoln throughout unusually grave and calm,
quite a different man from his normal self, sitting with an
air of dignity in his chair instead of lolling about in the
most ungainly attitudes, as his invariable custom was.
Later Mr Stanton, on leaving the council with the
Attorney-General, said to the latter, "That is the most
satisfactory cabinet meeting I have attended for many a
long day!
What an extraordinary change in Mr Lincoln!" The
Attorney-General replied, "We all saw it, before you
came
in. While we were waiting for you, he said, with his chin

down on his breast, 'Gentlemen, something very extraordinary is going to happen, and that very soon.'"
To which the Attorney-General had observed, "Something good, sir, I hope?" when the President answered very gravely: "I don't know; I don't know. But it will happen, and shortly too! ... I have had a dream. And I have now had the same dream three times. Once, on the night preceding the Battle of Bull Run. Once, on the night preceding –" (and
he named such another a battle also not favourable to the North.) ... His chin sank on his breast again, and he sat reflecting. "Might one ask the nature of this dream, sir?" said the Attorney-General. "Well," replied the President, without lifting his head or changing his attitude, "I am on a great broad rolling river – and I am in a boat – and I drift – and I drift! – but this is not business"
– suddenly raising
his face and looking round the table as Mr Stanton entered,
"let us proceed to business, gentlemen." Mr Stanton and the Attorney-General said, as they walked on together, it would be curious to notice whether anything ensued on this, and they agreed to notice. President Lincoln was shot that night.

On the 7th of February – my 56th birthday – I finally had my interview with his successor, President Johnson. Each of us looked at the other very hard, but I would have picked him out anywhere. A man of very remarkable appearance indeed, of tremendous firmness of purpose.
Not to be turned or trifled with. A man, I should say, who – like his predecessor – must needs be killed to be got out
of the way...

We moved on to Baltimore and a bright responsive people, very pleasant to read to... Baltimore, when first we came, had been snowing hard for four and twenty hours, though the place is as far south as Valencia in Spain. Here the ghost of slavery still haunted the houses though now the old, untidy, incapable, lounging, shambling black served you as a "free man". During the recent war between North and South it is said the ladies used to spit when they passed a Northern soldier. They are very handsome women, with an Eastern touch in them, and dress brilliantly – a striking contrast, I found, with towns such as Buffalo near the frontier.

It is my experience that in Buffalo American female beauty dies out...

Dolby and Osgood, meanwhile, continued to "train for the match", once again proving themselves ludicrous beyond belief. I would spy them coming up the street – each trying to pass the other – and immediately flee. I would sit down in my hotel-room to write a letter and they would burst in at the door and sit down on the floor to "blow", as they put it. When Dolby then sat down to write a letter at a neighbouring table, his bald head would smoke as if he were on fire.

One day being bright and cool, I took Dolby for a "buster" (as they put it) of eight miles. As everybody in New York seemed to know me, the spectacle of our splitting up the fashionable avenue (the only way out of town) excited the greatest amazement.

Back in Boston itself I had got to know *Christmas Carol*
so well that I couldn't – so to speak – remember it and occasionally went dodging about in the wildest manner to pick up lost pieces. One night they took it so tremendously I was stopped every five minutes. One poor young girl dressed in mourning clothes burst into a passion of grief about Tiny Tim, and had to be taken out...

Finally it was Saturday 29th February, and the great day of the Boston walking-match had at last arrived.
It was still over tremendously difficult ground, against a biting wind and through deep snow-wreaths. It was so cold, too, that our hair, beards, eyelashes and eyebrows were frozen hard and hung with icicles. The course was thirteen miles... The two performers had not the faintest notion of the weight of the task they had undertaken. Each would endeavour to persuade the other to take something unwholesome before starting.

At the halfway turning-point the two of them were close together, when Osgood suddenly went ahead at a splitting pace and with extraordinary endurance, winning by half a mile. Dolby did very well indeed and begged that, as loser, he might not be despised... We were not *quite* determined whether our friend Mrs Fields – wife of my American publisher – did not desert our colours by coming on the ground in a carriage, and having bread soaked in brandy put into the winning man's mouth as
he (that is to say, Osgood) streamed along. She pleaded that she would have done as much for Dolby if *he* had been ahead, so we were inclined to forgive her... and that evening I gave a very splendid dinner: eighteen covers, most magnificent flowers and such table decoration as was never seen in these parts. The whole thing had proved a great success, with everybody delighted! I alone, perhaps, was the unlikely casualty: by the time I left America it would be with a "neuralgic infection of the right foot", occasioned – according to my American doctor – by great fatigue in the severe winter... and excessive walking.

Indeed the weather gave no sign of relenting. Before we struck out for our short tour north-west of smaller outlying places, it was telegraphed that the storm prevailed over an immense extent of country, the roads very bad and the trains out of time. I hoped it might prove a wind-up.

We were getting sick of the sound of sleigh-bells even...

Lights dim a little.

Continuing and Concluding Our Faithful Report Of The Memorable Trial Of Mrs Bardell Against Pickwick, The Former Sueing The Latter For Breach Of Promise In A Marriage-Understanding Between The Two Parties, And Ably Assisted And Abetted Therein By The Lawfirm of Messrs. Dodson and Fogg...

An anxious quarter of an hour elapsed; the jury came back; the judge was fetch in. Mr Pickwick put on his spectacles, and gazed at the foreman with an agitated countenance and a quickly beating heart.

"Gentlemen," said the individual in black, "are you all agreed upon your verdict?"

"We are," replied the foreman.

"Do you find for the plaintiff, gentlemen, or for the defendant?"

"For the plaintiff."

"With what damages, gentleman?"

"Seven hundred and fifty pounds."

Mr Pickwick took off his spectacles, carefully wiped the glasses, folded them into their case, and put them in his pocket; then having drawn on his gloves with great nicety, and stared at the foreman all the while, he mechanically followed Mr Perker and the blue bag out of court.

They stopped in a side room while Perker paid the court fees; and here, Mr Pickwick was joined by his friends. Here, too, he encountered Messrs. Dodson and Fogg, rubbing their hands with every token of outward satisfaction.

"Well, gentlemen," said Mr Pickwick.

"Well, sir," said Dodson: for self and partner.

"You imagine you'll get your costs, don't you, gentlemen?" said Mr Pickwick.

Fogg said they thought it rather probable. Dodson smiled, and said they'd try.

"You may try, and try, and try again, Messrs. Dodson and Fogg," said Mr Pickwick vehemently, "but not one farthing of costs or damages do you ever get from me, if I spend the rest of my existence in a debtor's prison."

"Ha, ha!" laughed Dodson. "You'll think better of that, before next term, Mr Pickwick."

"He, he, he! We'll soon see about that, Mr Pickwick," grinned Fogg.

Speechless with indignation, Mr Pickwick allowed himself to be led by his solicitor and friends to the door, and there assisted into a hackney-coach, which had been fetched for the purpose by the ever watchful Sam Weller.

Sam had put up the steps, and was preparing to jump upon the box, when he felt himself gently touched on the shoulder; and looking round, his father stood before him. The old gentleman's countenance wore a mournful expression, as he shook his head gravely, and said, in warning accents:

"I know'd what 'ud come o' this here mode o' doin' bisness. Oh Sammy, Sammy, vy worn't there a alleybi!"

Lights come up again.

The Trial of Mr Pickwick proved the most popular of all,
as we continued to blaze away at our readings – now in Rochester, Syracuse, Buffalo, Springfield, Utica, Portland, New Boston and elsewhere.

In Providence, so enthusiastic was the crowd I was marched up the steps of my hotel protected by two policemen – this, it struck me, was very like going into a police van in Bow Street.

Meanwhile, the thaw, continuing, had placed the whole country under water. By now I was growing very home-sick, very anxious for April, taking laudanum to sleep and against the pains of my foot, which had started to swell again...

At the Niagara Falls there is now a suspension bridge across, and another, already completed, was to be opened
a few months hence. These bridges were very fine but ticklish, hanging aloft there, in the continual vibration of the thundering water. Nor was one greatly reassured by
the printed notice that troops must not cross them at step, and that bands of music must not play in crossing...

I shall never forget the last moment in which we saw Niagara. As we stood watching it with our faces to the top
of the Falls, our backs were towards the sun. The majestic valley below, so seen through the vast cloud of spray, was made of rainbow, as were the high banks, the riven rocks, the forests, the bridge, the buildings, the air, the sky. Nothing in Turner's finest water-colour drawings, done in
his greatest day, is so ethereal, so imaginative, so gorgeous in colour, as what I then beheld. I seemed to be lifted from the earth and to be looking into Heaven; the "muddy vesture of our clay" fell from us as we looked...
I chartered
a separate carriage for our men, so that they might see all in their own way, and at their own time (this visit had been promised to them, as a treat) but – as for Dolby and me – we said to one another, "Let it evermore re-

main so" and shut our eyes and came away.

... But now there was a great deal of water out between us and New York (to which, by way of intervening towns, we were slowly returning): the whole country for three hundred miles was flooded – nothing to be seen but drowned farms, barns adrift like Noah's arks, deserted villages, broken bridges, and all manner of ruin – and we were only able to leave the town of Utica after our reading thanks to a hundred men in seven-league boots going ahead of the train, each armed with a long pole and pushing the blocks of ice away.

And now again – but for the final time – Boston, or (so familiar was it becoming) what some were beginning to call my "native place"...

Ladies and gentlemen, what with climate, distance, catarrh, travelling, and hard work, I was nearly used up. I was to give six last readings, and by the third a doctor told me not to perform. I did so nonetheless but, now enduring my sleepless nights and surviving only on soup or beef-tea, I was tremendously "beat". Henry Wadsworth Longfellow and all the Harvard men urged me to give in. That day I took a biscuit and sherry at twelve and then drank a pint of champagne at three. When the evening
came I read as I never had before, and astonished the audience quite as much as myself: you never heard such a scene of excitement. Afterwards – and after every reading that week – I lay on the sofa for full thirty minutes in a
state of the greatest exhaustion, unable even to change out of my clothes.

Two snowstorms blotted the town out in a ceaseless whirl of snow and wind... Dolby proved as tender as a woman and as watchful as a doctor. He never left me during the readings, now, but sat at the

side of the platform and kept his eye upon me all the time. To conclude I gave them *Dombey* one night; *Dr Marigold*
and *Martin Chuzzlewit* the next. Returning to the platform after prolonged applause, I bade the good people of Boston farewell; their personal affection for me was charming to the last.

Now there was only New York. Imagine me, if you will, lame and hobbling, leaning on Dolby or others kind enough to assist, unable now even to fit a boot on my foot, which finds itself swathed – for want of a gout-stocking – in something best resembling a carpet-bag, afraid all this time that the news of my illness would be telegraphed back to London, thereby alarming my family and my beloved...
I gave my last five readings, concluding with *A Christmas Carol* and the trial scene from *Pickwick Papers*.

At the farewell banquet held for me at Delmonico's more than two hundred had been invited...

Lights dim a little.

Ladies and gentlemen, it is invariably sad to do something for the last time... The shadow of one word – "goodbye" – has impended over me all this evening. When I was reading to you from *David Copperfield* last Thursday night, I felt that there was more than usual significance for me in the declaration of Mr Peggotty: "My future life lies over the sea"...

I henceforth charge myself to express my high and grateful sense of my second reception in America, and to bear my honest testimony to the national generosity and magnanimity. Also to record that whenever I have been, in the smallest places equally with the largest, I have been received with unsurpassable politeness, decency, sweet temper, hospitality and consideration.

I was asked in this very city of New York, about last Christmas-time, whether an American was not at some disadvantage in England as a foreigner. The notion of an American being regarded in England as a foreigner at all, of his ever being thought of or spoken of in that character, was so uncommonly incongruous and absurd to me that my gravity was, for the moment, quite overpowered... As soon as it was restored I said that it was my unvarying experience that it was enough in England to be an American to be received with the readiest respect and recognition anywhere. I am re- minded of a lady who, being in London, had a great desire to see the famous Reading Room of the British Museum, but was told that it was unfortunately impossible because the place was closed for a week. Upon her going – as she as- sured me – alone to the Museum, self-introduced as an *American* lady, the gate flew open as it were magically. (I am unwillingly bound to add that this young lady was extremely pretty – a fact that could certainly not have escaped the doorman...)

Points of difference there have been, points of difference there are. But I do believe from the great majority of honest minds on both sides there cannot be absent the conviction that it would be better for this globe to be ridden by an earthquake, fired by a comet, overrun by an iceberg, and abandoned to the Arctic fox and bear, than that it should present the spectacle of those two great nations, each of whom has, in its own way and hour, striven so hard and success- fully for freedom, ever again being arrayed the one against the other...

I entreat you to believe that in passing from

my sight you will not pass from my memory. I
shall often recall you as I see you now, equally by
my winter fire and in the green English summer
weather. I shall never recall you as a mere public
audience, but rather as a host of personal friends,
and ever with the greatest gratitude, tenderness
and consideration.

Ladies and gentlemen, I beg to bid you farewell. And I pray God bless you, and God bless
the land in which I have met you.

He holds the audience's gaze. Enormous offstage applause.

Lights full up again.

I had come out on the *Cuba*; I went home
on the *Russia* – sailing from New York Harbour
on April 22nd.

Only on the passage home to England, and
then some three days into the crossing, did my
cold, my "true American catarrh", turn faith-
less at last and leave me... whereupon a "depu-
tation" (two ladies in number, of whom only
one could get into my cabin while the other
looked in at my window) came to ask me if I
would be so kind as to read to the passengers
that evening in the saloon.

I had read four times a week, 76 times in
all, in churches, theatres, concert rooms and
lecture halls, over a period of more than four
months in all manner of towns. The profits had
been enormous – something over twenty thousand pounds. Illustrious novelist that I was, had
I not blazed across the North American continent? And was I not – after all – still "Boz", the
Inimitable? Would I not therefore "blaze" this
one last time?

Unconditionally and absolutely, I declined the good ladies' invitation – respectfully replying that, sooner than give even one more reading, I would assault the ship's captain and be put in irons!

Ladies and gentlemen, did I know already that I was drifting swiftly on my own broad and rolling river – and that this same river was bearing me to an Ocean greater yet than the Atlantic...?

That already the "Old, old fashion" – Death! – was coming in fast...?

Had I perceived that soon I would be confronted with My Maker, asking "Boz, what mean you by coming here at this time of day? Have you no... 'alleybi'?"

Beat.

I arrived back in England. On seeing me, my doctor recoiled, quite broken down in spirits.

"Good lord! Mr Dickens!" he said, "You look seven years younger!"

He smiles, nods and finally bows his head.

Lights dim slowly to blackout.

End of the Play.